# Seeking Intimacy in a Diverse Community

**Other books by Phyllis K. Peterson**

*Assisting the Traumatized Soul: Healing the Wounded Talisman*
*Healing the Wounded Soul*
*The Heroic Female Spirit*
*Remaining Faithful*

# Seeking Intimacy
## in a
# Diverse Community

Seeking the Spiritual Reality of the Mentally Ill,
the Physically Challenged and the Emotionally Wounded

by

Phyllis K. Peterson

GR

George Ronald
Oxford

George Ronald, *Publisher*
Oxford
www.grbooks.com

*A catalogue record for this book is available
from the British Library*

ISBN 978–0–85398–575–4

Cover design: Steiner Graphics

# Contents

*This book is dedicated to all those*
*who feel the stigma of being different,*
*who have been misunderstood, bullied, and neglected.*
*May they find acceptance and support*
*as others come to believe in their spiritual reality.*
*It is also dedicated to their caregivers*
*who have sometimes been so stressed to their last limits*
*that their only relief has been tearful prayers to God.*
*May they seek out resources in their community*
*that can provide knowledge and choices.*

# Acknowledgements

There are so many people I would like to thank who provided the stories that resulted in this book. However, I cannot name them out of respect for their privacy. Names, locations and situations have been changed to protect them.

I drew inspiration from my friend, Kim Babb, who works with autistic children in a school setting. He asked me to call attention to the suffering of the mentally ill in our community because he observed the frustration of the Bahá'í community that was bereft of the knowledge of how to act. Without his deep concern continually motivating me, I doubt that I could have finished writing this book. I also wish to acknowledge my publisher, George Ronald, and my editors for helping this book attain its highest possibilities. May it be a port in the storms we all face in life.

# Preface

When I was on pilgrimage in late 2004 a pilgrim asked a Counsellor member of the International Teaching Centre what she should do about the three mentally ill members of her study circle. The response was to consult with her assembly and/or auxiliary board member. Another pilgrim from another area tried to raise the concern again. And again the Counsellor responded the same way.

The issue of mental health has also been a concern in our community. A facilitator from our area started a new Book One study circle with twelve new non-Bahá'í participants and of these twelve, three had serious mental health issues that interfered with the course of the study. A discussion was held about whether or not to isolate the ill people.

In a recent teacher training seminar at the junior high school where I work, the school psychologist stood up and said that there is not a single person in the room who is not touched by mental illness. He himself had a brother with schizophrenia and two uncles who were alcoholics. The emphasis in this seminar was on education regarding the stigmas and identification of mental illness.

If we Bahá'ís are to have entry by troops, we will need to address the needs of the mentally ill. If the Faith has room for everyone, then it has room for the mentally ill. Many assemblies and board members will be very helpful in the process in dealing with this population. But most assemblies will probably not be able to respond to the needs that accompany mental illness and this may result in the new seekers and believers being alienated and shunned and lead to them turning away from the Faith. It appears that what is needed is information about how to be intimate with those who have special needs, whose stress levels in the community increase and who create stress for other members of the community.

Auxiliary board members, their assistants and local spiritual assemblies need to have some understanding of therapy. Our communities need to be prepared for an influx of people with various degrees of mental illness. Education of the Bahá'ís in accommodation of the mentally ill will go a long way in creating a community that is welcoming and an integral part in the healing and comfort of many of these people. Here is where we need to change.[1] Of those mentally ill individuals who are attracted to the Faith, most are being treated by professionals and are on maintenance medications, so it is not a matter of simply referring them to professionals for care. It is clearly a case that we must, through community education, make a place where all are welcome, a place where spiritual education and healing can take place.

*Kim Babb*[2]

# Dance of Intimacy

My community has had a disruptive person in the past.

The woman did find some solace and acceptance in the Bahá'í community even though she was incredibly hostile and would shriek in a torrent of negativity at the slightest perceived offence. Trust was a very difficult issue for her. She really responded when I told her dying mother that I thought her daughter was a wonderful woman. There was so much estrangement among her family members.

There was a time when I desperately wanted to go to a programme at the House of Worship and she wanted to go with me. I picked her up and she said she had something that had to be done to her car at her service garage. So we went in her car. Then she said she had to pick up a few groceries. Following that she had to drop something off on the other side of town. Then she had to mail something. With each task I practised patience. Finally we started off on our trip to the House of Worship and I knew there was no chance that we would arrive on time. We were going to miss the programme and I was a little sad as well as disappointed. But we went anyway and I didn't tell her about my misgivings.

When we got there, we found out that the programme had been delayed for an hour and a half because the speaker was late! So I got to see the entire programme! And learned a big lesson in patience and realized that God was really guiding my friend into learning to trust me.

I kept a friendship with her for a year (which, she said, she had never managed to maintain with anyone else), until

I, too, became offensive to 'her'. She then left the Faith and moved to another state. It broke my heart when she left the Faith. I sobbed and sobbed at Feast while I told the story of how I had offended her, which in reality left her friendless. I'm hoping she tried the Bahá'í community in the next city that she moved to and that she progressed.

ళ

This is a story of extreme patience and selflessness. It describes a dance of intimacy with a mentally ill person leading as the evening evolved. The woman who was led remained open to change at every turn, not knowing where or when it would end, but openness and forbearance were her virtues. How many of us would have been that open – that uncontrolling, that trusting? And, how do we prepare for such a diverse community that will include the mentally ill, the physically challenged, a variety of ethnicities and the wounded?

## A Growing Description of Our Bahá'í Community

We have a community of educated and uneducated, professional and non-professional people. We are wounded, mentally ill and healthy; moral, obedient and edified; and there exists within our body of believers those who are striving to become whole through a maintenance programme of medication and support groups plus those who are determined to become moral through obedience to Bahá'u'lláh. Some of us have lost every material thing we've ever owned; some of us have every material thing we need. Some of the educated need to develop character and some of the uneducated are on a higher spiritual level.

Yet all of us are called to a higher purpose than our own individual development, to achieve oneness and unity amongst this diverse community through virtues bestowed by the Holy

Spirit. We are a community that is learning to develop true intimacy through our devotional meetings, reflection meetings and home visits. And we must learn somehow to continue to integrate not only the races but those who are outcast because of mental illness or physical disability.

The purpose of this book is to examine how we can create a greater intimacy that attracts souls and confirms them as we welcome large numbers into our community – large numbers that include those who suffer from differing degrees of mental illness and those of us who have preconceived notions about the wounded and do not know how to welcome them into our circles:

By the same token, desire and willingness to open certain aspects of community life to the wider public should be integrated into a pattern of behaviour that attracts souls and confirms them. Much has been achieved in this respect as the friends have adopted new ways of thinking and acting at a collective level. In welcoming large numbers into its embrace, the community is learning to see more readily the latent potentiality in people and to avoid setting artificial barriers for them based on preconceived notions. A nurturing environment is being cultivated in which each individual is encouraged to progress at his or her own pace without the pressure of unreasonable expectations. At the heart of such developments is a growing awareness of the implications of the universality and comprehensiveness of the Faith. Collective action is governed more and more by the principle that Bahá'u'lláh's message should be given liberally and unconditionally to humanity. Most gratifying are the endeavours being made to reach receptive populations with the teachings of the Faith. As unrelenting social and political forces continue to uproot people from their homelands and sweep them across continents, an uncompromising appreciation for a diversity of backgrounds and for the strength it confers on the whole will prove crucial to the expansion and consolidation of the community.[3]

This was the hope and urging of Shoghi Effendi, who wrote of 'the highly diversified Bahá'í society of the future'[4] and, urging the Bahá'ís to pay special attention to winning the adherence to the Faith of different races, wrote:

A blending of these highly differentiated elements of the human race, harmoniously interwoven into the fabric of an all-embracing Bahá'í fraternity, and assimilated through the dynamic processes of a divinely appointed Administrative Order, and contributing each its share to the enrichment and glory of Bahá'í community life, is surely an achievement the contemplation of which must warm and thrill every Bahá'í heart.[5]

This Faith, Shoghi Effendi wrote, 'does not ignore, nor does it attempt to suppress, the diversity of ethnical origins, of climate, of history, of language and tradition, of thought and habit, that differentiate the peoples and nations of the world'.[6]

Though this speaks to an ideal, the National Spiritual Assembly of the United States was wise enough to note that oneness also includes people of special needs:

As larger numbers of people become Bahá'ís, the institutions as well as individual believers will have to learn to accommodate and to assist those persons who may or may not be mentally ill by medical definition but, nonetheless, have negative, unpleasant or disruptive personalities. When a believer has emotional or psychological problems which render him incapable of behaving responsibly, the Local Spiritual Assembly must, to safeguard the welfare of the community, consider what it can do to minimize the person's influence. On the one hand it must endeavour to help such persons

4

face their challenges in life, which may be considerable, and develop their God-given spiritual potential, and at the same time protect the community from disruption and divisiveness.[7]

We may question: How can we attempt to enter the reality of such a diverse international mixture of people, 'people of divers beliefs, of conflicting creeds, and opposing temperaments'?[8]

But the secret lies in Bahá'u'lláh's call to oneness. It also lies hidden in the heart of every soul created by God. Each heart whether of the whole and healthy or the mentally ill hungers for intimacy, unity and oneness, and the Word of God fosters its development and growth.

> Every verse which this Pen hath revealed is a bright and shining portal that discloseth the glories of a saintly and pious life, of pure and stainless deeds. The summons and the message which We gave were never intended to reach or to benefit one land or one people only. Mankind in its entirety must firmly adhere to whatsoever hath been revealed and vouchsafed unto it. Then and only then will it attain unto true liberty.[9]

We shall start anew every day as thousands of diverse peoples join Ruhi study circles for the first time and learn the teachings of Bahá'u'lláh. And what power will hold us together in our differences as we work towards world peace and unity? Our beloved Master, 'Abdu'l-Bahá, makes clear:

> . . . a power above and beyond the powers of nature must needs be brought to bear, to change this black darkness into light, and these hatreds and resentments, grudges and spites, these endless wrangles and wars, into fellowship and love amongst all the peoples of the earth. This power is none

other than the breathings of the Holy Spirit and the mighty inflow of the Word of God.[10]

We shall see, in the following stories, examples of confirmation from the Holy Spirit as each individual is guided from fear and fantasy to concrete assistance to those who are in dire need.

Story 2

# Deepening Trust

James was walking with a cynical heart and with 'resentment and grudges' against a family member until 'Abdu'l-Bahá and Bahá'u'lláh brightened his pathway with the Word of God, changing his heart, which was locked.

> The Word of God is the king of words and its pervasive influence is incalculable. It hath ever dominated and will continue to dominate the realm of being. The Great Being saith: The Word is the master key for the whole world, inasmuch as through its potency the doors of the hearts of men, which in reality are the doors of heaven, are unlocked. No sooner had but a glimmer of its effulgent splendour shone forth upon the mirror of love than the blessed word 'I am the Best-Beloved' was reflected therein. It is an ocean inexhaustible in riches, comprehending all things. Every thing which can be perceived is but an emanation therefrom. High, immeasurably high is this sublime station, in whose shadow moveth the essence of loftiness and splendour, wrapt in praise and adoration.[11]

James got a call from his brother, Mark, who told him that he needed help because his car had stalled 50 miles out of town when he had taken another brother, George, out to a fishing spot. They had got a ride back home from a stranger named Keith, who had taken his golf bag out of his back seat and put it in his trunk so Mark and George could sit in the car. When they got home, George's wallet was missing and he assumed it was in the back seat of the stranger's car.

George has been diagnosed with schizophrenia. He hears the voice of the devil and says, 'I rebuke you, I rebuke you!' hundreds of times non-stop, daily. Both Mark and George lived hard lives with drugs and alcohol for over 40 years but have been 'clean' for ten years. They both attend a Christian church and read their Bible and pray regularly. James is a Bahá'í and has always been there for his brothers but this situation was causing him some doubt.

James had no definite destination other than 40 to 50 miles out of town. He had no last name of the stranger. He had no address, just sketchy landmarks like 'a quarry in the vicinity'. But he agreed to start off on this 'adventure', praying that he would be guided to find his brother's car.

With Mark giving him directions, James found the quarry and the car. The car even started but there was no clue as to who the stranger was.

Down the road from the quarry and car was a gas station. They stopped there and asked if someone there knew a 'Keith' who played golf. No one knew Keith but another clerk was going to arrive soon, so they waited to ask her.

Tamara arrived after ten minutes. She knew a 'Keith' who played golf and told the brothers how to get to the golf course. Mark couldn't remember the directions (he has problems with his memory owing to his past alcohol and drug addiction) but James could . . . even though Mark kept telling him he was going in the wrong direction. James kept 'checking' his doubt.

James found the golf course. Mark told him that he would do the talking. He didn't want to give out too much information about the wallet because there were a couple of hundred dollars in it. Mark inquired at the desk if there was someone named 'Keith' who played golf there. The people at the desk were reluctant to give out information to such rough looking characters. James kept saying the 'Remover of Difficulties' silently. Mark explained the situation to the receptionist. Finally the clerk called a 'Keith' who turned out to be the wrong person. James and his brothers decided to return home.

The next day the Keith who had picked up Mark and George played golf and was told that three men were looking for him because one of them had left his wallet in the back seat of his car. Keith looked for the wallet and found it. He also found George's ID card with his address. He then drove 50 miles out of his way to George's home and returned the wallet intact!

∾

This is an example of the working of the Holy Spirit and the Word of God in receptive souls. It shows how God works to protect the weak and indigent, not only in the Bahá'í community but in the Christian community and other religious communities.

> O Son of Spirit! Vaunt not thyself over the poor, for I lead him on his way and behold thee in thy evil plight and confound thee for evermore.[12]

If James had not been merciful, he could not have been an agent of change for his brothers. And if he had not studied the Word of God every day, he would not have known how to be of service to his brothers. James used the virtues of faith, love for his brothers, mercy, understanding and compassion for their condition and his intuition to help his brothers.

> The Holy Word has been extolled by the Prophets of God as the medium of celestial power and the wellspring of all spiritual, social and material progress. Access to it, constant study of it and daily use of it in our individual lives are vital

to the inner personal transformation towards which we strive
and whose ultimate outer manifestation will be the emer-
gence of that divine civilization which is the promise of the
World Order of Bahá'u'lláh . . .[13]

James also had to 'suspend judgement'. We are not therapists
or psychiatrists but if we rely on the biblical teaching of 'Do
not judge, or you too will be judged' (Matthew 7:1, NIV),
then we can truly suspend judgement. James lived a 'Seven
Valleys' moment: he did not depend upon acquired knowledge and book learning but 'crossed the water':

The story is told of a mystic knower, who went on a journey
with a learned grammarian as his companion. They came to
the shore of the Sea of Grandeur. The knower straightway
flung himself into the waves, but the grammarian stood lost
in his reasonings, which were as words that are written on
water. The knower called out to him, 'Why dost thou not
follow?' The grammarian answered, 'O Brother, I dare not
advance. I must needs go back again.' Then the knower cried,
'Forget what thou didst read in the books of Sibavayh and
Qawlavayh, of Ibn-i-Hájib and Ibn-i-Málik [famed writers
on grammar and rhetoric] and cross the water.'

  The death of self is needed here, not rhetoric:
  Be nothing, then, and walk upon the waves. [*Mathnaví*][14]

Rainer Maria Rilke writes:

But only someone who is ready for everything, who doesn't
exclude any experience, even the most incomprehensible,
will live the relationship with another person as something
alive and will himself sound the depths of his own being.[15]

We must not think of transformation in the context only

of those who are immoral or uneducated or those who are mentally ill or wounded, but in the context that ALL of us as human beings have been commanded by Bahá'u'lláh to develop virtues that will help us to advance civilization.

A vast spectrum of humanity is going to enter the Bahá'í community. The community is open unconditionally to anyone who believes in Bahá'u'lláh and sincerely wants to follow His teachings. Some people wishing to be part of the community will be mentally ill.

One report regarding the devastation of hurricane Katrina in 2005 said that out of the million and a half people affected, a hundred thousand were bi-polar and had difficulty getting their medication. Had this number included Bahá'ís, how would we have responded to their needs? How would we have judged their behaviour and their symptoms?

Even among Bahá'ís, those with mental illnesses and physical disabilities are stigmatized.

But let's forget about labels such as mental illness, depression, bi-polar, schizophrenia and so on and bring the discussion back to the basics that 'Abdu'l-Bahá has taught us: that each of us has a higher/spiritual nature and a lower/physical nature, which puts us all on the same level.

## 'Abdu'l-Bahá on the Two Natures of Mankind

We must care for man's two natures; for as the material man makes certain demands for food and raiment and if not looked after suffers, even so his spiritual reality suffers without care. This is why the divine messengers come to the rescue – to care for the reality, that man's thoughts may unfold and his aims become realized, that he many inherit a new field of progress, for the spiritual side should be cared for as much as the corporeal; the help that comes is through the resuscitating breath of the Holy Spirit.[16]

To care for the 'spiritual reality' of another we have to depend upon the Holy Spirit's guidance in preparation, in the moment, and in happily bringing ourselves to account for the greater good we have completed. If we do this, we will be acting from our own 'spiritual reality'. This is a key factor because we can seek the spiritual reality of another only when we are acting from our own spiritual reality. Our spiritual reality is expressed by the utilization of our virtues that are granted by the Holy Spirit.

> In man there are two natures; his spiritual or higher nature and his material or lower nature. In one he approaches God, in the other he lives for the world alone. Signs of both these natures are to be found in men. In his material aspect he expresses untruth, cruelty and injustice; all these are the outcome of his lower nature. The attributes of his Divine nature are shown forth in love, mercy, kindness, truth and justice, one and all being expressions of his higher nature. Every good habit, every noble quality belongs to man's spiritual nature, whereas all his imperfections and sinful actions are born of his material nature. If a man's Divine nature dominates his human nature, we have a saint.[17]

It's easy to show love, mercy and kindness to those who 'fit' into our community. But what about the dirty, the smelly, the uncouth, those who are still racist or sexist, those who dominate the consultation, the irreverent who may also be receptive to the Revelation of Bahá'u'lláh? Will we love them and invite them into our community too?

Story 3

# An Example of Faithfulness

Shohreh, a Bahá'í in her seventies, is very concerned about her brother, who is failing in his health. The following is just an example of three days of her trying to assist him under extreme conditions.

## Day 1

My brother, Rahmin, was in the hospital three months ago. His muscles were breaking down because he was severely dehydrated, which endangered his *one* kidney. He was also falling down because he had no muscular support. To further stabilize him, after three weeks of hospitalization he was placed at a care centre where he received good care and good meals, his medications were monitored and his condition improved.

He is now suffering a relapse and is, I believe, dehydrated again, which could explain why his muscles cannot support him anymore. He is complaining of a cramp in his left thigh, which relates, I think, to dehydration.

I spent two hours tonight with Rahmin. He had nothing to eat or drink all day. He cannot stand up without falling down. I fed him, I gave him some water to drink and listened to his confused speech as he hallucinated. He could not sit up in his recliner but kept falling out the side of it. He kept dropping his sandwich in the chair and on the floor. He fell down in the bathroom yesterday and the toilet tank broke apart, with water everywhere. He is not even able to put a frozen dinner into the microwave, let alone carry it to his chair to eat it, without dropping it. I told him that if he is not better by tomorrow when I come at 9 a.m., I am calling an ambulance to get him to the emergency room. I believe that this is the next step to getting him into a nursing home/rehab centre where he can be cared for as his condition continues to decline. I probably should have called an ambulance tonight but I want to give him notice of what I am going to do. He is beyond whatever I can do to help him now. I am very tired and under great duress. The stench in his apartment is getting to me – and to his landlord who asked him, 'How can you live like this?' The cockroaches had been so bad they were falling in his food when he tried to eat. I called an exterminator.

## Day 2

Well, I missed my opportunity. I fed him and gave him water last night and he's better today because he had some nourishment. I'll wait to determine whether that was the answer to our prayers. He looks pretty darn rough, blood all over his T-shirt. The shake I bought him last night has run down his shirt.

He greeted me last night and this morning in his underwear and told me he's not going to the hospital. He's still got some fight left in him. He says if he goes in, he'll never get out again. And I know that's true.

He knows he's going down and if I let him, he'll take me down too. So, I'm backing off for now until either I get my strength back or he has another emergency like last night.

Today I watched him pick up his chewing tobacco which had spilled all over the floor and put it in his mouth. He chewed it for a minute or two and then I watched him take it out and start pulling long hairs out of it. I felt sick to my stomach.

He's walking and sitting more upright today and that's the only good sign. His medicine was all over the floor this morning and I don't know if he's taking too much or too little.

I asked him if he could get his pants on and if he could change his shirt. He said, 'Yes.' He then asked if I was going to call the police on him. I said, 'Not today.' He's wary of me.

## Day 3

My other brother, who has a disability, called and asked me to check on Rahmin. He wants me to go over and check on him every day. I told him I was weak physically today and couldn't do it. He said, 'If you give me a ride over there, I'll spend the day with him.' Another answer to prayer and blessed relief for me. The tension in my rib cage was very strong yesterday.

❧

It is clear that Shohreh needs to check in with a Visiting Nurses Association to get advice and an assessment of her brother, which she knows he would refuse. She also needs support, not only from her community but also from a support group of those who are in her shoes. She is a very giving person and has her own difficulties with ageing. She is always asking herself if her brother is going to be dead by the time she gets to his apartment to help him and it is a terrible burden for her. But she steels herself like a good soldier and walks the path of loving-kindness, tolerance and compassion. She has seen her brother's spiritual beauty from childhood and keeps those realities and memories in her heart.

Know that there are two natures in man: the physical nature and the spiritual nature. The physical nature is inherited from Adam, and the spiritual nature is inherited from the Reality of the Word of God, which is the spirituality of Christ. The physical nature is born of Adam, but the spiritual nature is born from the bounty of the Holy Spirit. The first is the source of all imperfection; the second is the source of all perfection.[18]

The Holy Spirit did guide Shohreh to seek out help and keep faith with her brother and the system. She took on the challenging tasks of gathering a work crew, emptying Rahmin's roach-filled apartment, saving his clean clothing, finding a wheelchair for him and locating an apartment that was clean and worthy of a human being. Lastly, she replaced his furniture, which was filled with cockroaches. In reality, not all of us could stretch ourselves to this extent but Shohreh could sacrifice and did. Friends and relatives helped. Today Rahmin has overcome most of his physical difficulties and is living safely on his own.

What other virtues did the Holy Spirit grant to Shohreh? How did she act from her spiritual reality?

We, of course, have an important example from the story of Lua Getsinger in Howard Colby Ives's book *Portals to Freedom*:

As I write there is brought to memory a story told by Lua Getsinger, she who then sat in the audience before me. In the very early days of the knowledge of the Cause of Bahá'u'lláh in America Mrs. Getsinger was in 'Akká having made the pilgrimage to the prison city to see the Master. She was with Him one day when He said to her, that He was too busy today to call upon a friend of His who was very ill and poor and He wished her to go in His place. Take him food and care for him as I have been doing, He concluded. He told her where this man was to be found and she went gladly, proud that 'Abdu'l-Bahá should trust her with this mission.

She returned quickly. 'Master,' she exclaimed, 'surely you

cannot realize to what a terrible place you sent me. I almost fainted from the awful stench, the filthy rooms, the degrading condition of that man and his house. I fled lest I contract some terrible disease.'

Sadly and sternly 'Abdu'l-Bahá regarded her. 'Dost thou desire to serve God,' He said, 'serve thy fellow man for in him dost thou see the image and likeness of God.' He told her to go back to this man's house. If it is filthy she should clean it; if this brother of yours is dirty, bathe him; if he is hungry, feed him. Do not return until this is done. Many times had He done this for him and cannot she serve him once?[19]

Note the 'clarifier' at the end of this quotation:

The imperfect members of society, the weak souls in humanity, follow their natural trend. Their lives and actions are in accord with their natural propensities; they are captives of physical susceptibilities; they are not in touch or in tune with the spiritual bounties. Man has two aspects: the physical, which is subject to nature, and the merciful or divine, which is connected with God. If the physical or natural disposition in him should overcome the heavenly and merciful, he is, then, the most degraded of animal beings; and if the divine and spiritual should triumph over the human and natural, he is, verily, an angel. The Prophets come into the world to guide and educate humanity so that the animal nature of man may disappear and the divinity of his powers become awakened. The divine aspect or spiritual nature consists of the breaths of the Holy Spirit. The second birth of which Jesus has spoken refers to the appearance of this heavenly nature in man. It is expressed in the baptism of the Holy Spirit, and he who is baptized by the Holy Spirit is a veritable manifestation of divine mercy to mankind. Then he becomes just and kind to all humanity; he entertains prejudice and ill will toward none; he shuns no nation or people.[20]

'Abdu'l-Bahá is not talking about mental illness in these statements – He is talking about all of us. Surely the mentally ill have a spiritual nature too – a spiritual reality. God knows His creation. The Hidden Words of Bahá'u'lláh were revealed for all of us and we are each accountable to develop virtues regardless of our condition when we enter the Faith, virtues such as understanding and compassion for those who are mentally ill.

We are informed by 'Abdu'l-Bahá that:

God has created all, and all return to God. Therefore, love humanity with all your heart and soul. If you meet a poor man, assist him; if you see the sick, heal him; reassure the affrighted one, render the cowardly noble and courageous, educate the ignorant, associate with the stranger. Emulate God. Consider how kindly, how lovingly He deals with all, and follow His example. You must treat people in accordance with the divine precepts – in other words, treat them as kindly as God treats them, for this is the greatest attainment possible for the world of humanity.[21]

The only real difference that exists between people is that they are at various stages of development. Some are imperfect – these must be brought to perfection. Some are asleep – they must be awakened; some are negligent – they must be roused; but one and all are the children of God. Love them all with your whole heart; no one is a stranger to the other, all are friends.[22]

At most it is this: that some are ignorant; they must be educated in order that they may become intelligent. Some are immature as children; they must be aided and assisted in order that they may become mature. Some are sick and ailing; they must be healed. But the suffering patient must not be tested by false treatment. The child must not be warped and hindered in its development. The ignorant must not be restricted by censure and criticism. We must look for the real, true remedy.[23]

Therefore, no one should glorify himself over another; no one should manifest pride or superiority toward another; no one should look upon another with scorn and contempt; and no one should deprive or oppress a fellow creature. All must be considered as submerged in the ocean of God's mercy. We must associate with all humanity in gentleness and kindliness. We must love all with love of the heart. Some are ignorant; they must be trained and educated. One is sick; he must be healed. Another is as a child; we must assist him to attain maturity. We must not detest him who is ailing, neither shun him, scorn nor curse him, but care for him with the utmost kindness and tenderness. An infant must not be treated with disdain simply because it is an infant. Our responsibility is to train, educate and develop it in order that it may advance toward maturity.[24]

Some of the mentally ill are angry and they anger others. You may see them bully others verbally. This is learned behaviour as well as behaviour that shows they may feel threatened in the community. Some have no boundaries and are in danger. How are we to deal with this? How are we to respond when their behaviour is unjust? Can we separate behaviour from the man or woman? Can we take them aside privately to name the behaviour rather than shame them in front of a group? And is even this gesture going to be perceived as criticism? 'Abdu'l-Bahá says that we, too, must be educated. Recognizing that we need education can be a humbling experience for a Bahá'í who has been walking a spiritual path for many years.

Story 4

# Unending Frustration

Daniella said, 'I'm "wrapped" fairly. We've just returned from Feast, which we hosted at our sweet little Bahá'í centre.

'There is a Bahá'í in our community who has major mental health challenges. From the time we arrived, she was quiet for only a few seconds – okay, she was respectful during the devotional part. The rest of the time she dominated all conversation, consultation as well as during the social portion.

'I honestly felt like my head was going to explode. I worked very hard to maintain my composure. After everyone else had gone, she started to talk about how fat she is. That was just too much. I told her how hurt I'd been for 35 years when she complained about being fat – that I'd been three times her size and it was like a slap in the face. After having known someone for 35 years, this wasn't the first time I'd told her that. She thanked me for the feedback. I know she has no malice in her heart but has mental health issues that render her unable to think of anything other than herself and her burdens.

'How do you handle folks like this? It is so hard. Her behaviour is so outrageous that I don't want to have her around if I am ever able to get someone to actually come to a fireside. She has alienated a number of folks from the Faith.

'Her daughter lives in the next community and is more disturbed than her mother. Our assembly will not allow her to attend functions in this community. Tonight the mother wanted to discuss allowing her daughter to attend the cluster reflection meeting that is being held in a rented facility in our community but is being hosted by the daughter's community. I wanted to rip my already short hair out!'

౿ఎ

The woman in this story resorted to speaking the truth about her feelings and was able to get acknowledgment from the person who was a challenge to her. She revealed her frustration and concern because she didn't know how to handle the situation. But she was also using the virtue of 'truthfulness' to which the person did respond. In addition, she revealed compassion for the person.

Some of the notes in the Appendix address this type of challenge. The local spiritual assembly is rightly addressing the difficult situation and is setting appropriate limits.

## Nurture/Nature/Obedience

If we have not been nurtured with love or in the Word of God, we may struggle to react positively to the many tests we experience, relying on instinct rather than virtues in our responses.

When we become Bahá'ís we have the opportunity to be nurtured in a community based on the Word of God. We learn to take responsibility for all our behaviour, to bring ourselves to account each day, to choose obedience to God and His institutions of authority on earth, and to develop virtues with the help of the Holy Spirit.

The following table illustrates the contrast between 'Love, Compassion and Detachment' and the negative feelings and thoughts we might have that prevent us from operating from our higher nature, our spiritual reality, when we are faced with the challenge of the mentally ill.

You can refer to this table as a path that leads upward from feelings of negativity to love, compassion and detachment and the rest of the virtues.

Love and virtues are like an umbrella that embraces all our feelings so that they can be directed and regulated by our higher, spiritual nature. If our feelings are directed by passion, idle fancies and vain imaginings, we will fall into our lower nature, which is capable of oppression or judgmentalism.

# LOVE, COMPASSION AND DETACHMENT

## VIRTUES (Spiritual Reality)

Trustworthiness Truthfulness Helpfulness Faithfulness Discipline Confidence Consideration
Courage Obedience Orderliness Patience Peacefulness Prayerfulness Mercy Moderation Modesty Loyalty
Purposefulness Enthusiasm Determination Respect Responsibility Flexibility Forgiveness Reliability
Reverence Service Steadfastness Tact Honesty Thankfulness Tolerance Honour Courtesy Generosity

### POSITIVE FEELINGS

Comfortable Confident Enthusiastic Ardent Earnest Grateful Pleased Cheerful Buoyant Intuitive Elated Inspired Peaceful Optimistic
Trusting Merciful Determined Willing Fearless Courageous Contented Relaxed Calm Centred Friendly Hopeful Concerned Compassionate
Empathetic Uplifting Detached Tactful Committed Nurturing Empowered Empowering Curious Inquisitive Sincere Creative Humble
Cooperative Passionate Secure Bold Reassuring

### MEDITATIONS AND POSITIVE THOUGHTS

Problem-solving questions: How can I help create a support group for this person? What resources are there in the
community for this person? What do the writings say about the weak, sick, imperfect and those who need nurturing? How far can I extend myself without feeling resentful?
What virtue can I develop if I am feeling resentful? What help can I enlist in TEAM accompaniment for this person? Who can I consult with? If I say no or an immediate
request, could I tell him/her exactly when I could fill that request? Can I set boundaries with this person without excluding him/her from my life? How can I reorganize my
calendar to make a commitment to this individual? Which of my many faults should I work on now, rather than focusing on that person's inability to communicate their needs
and feelings? God, let me get beyond my need to criticize and instead acknowledge their need. Help me monitor my inconsistent feelings so I can act with purity of intention.

### NEGATIVE FEELINGS

Sorrowful Unhappy Depressed Melancholy Injured Isolated Offended Tortured Lonely Bitter Sceptical Suspicious Dubious Hopeless Powerless Pessimistic Resentful Irritated Enraged
Furious Annoyed Provoked Sullen Indignant Irate Wrathful Cross Confused Awkward Bewildered Fearful Worried Doubtful Hesitant Dismayed Cowardly Threatened Appalled Petrified
Gutless Cynical Hypocritical Bored Phoney Imposed-upon Condescending Inconsistent

## LOWER NATURE

I've got to worry about myself first. This is just too much trouble. I can't be bothered with this. I don't want to get involved. I'm not qualified to do this. Some people just don't have any
pride. I don't have the time to do this. Let his/her family take care of him/her. This person is too much of a risk. People have to pick themselves up by their bootstraps. If I let this person,
he/she could just take over my life. I have too much on my schedule to make another commitment. Getting involved would be too much of a sacrifice. I feel very afraid.

✌

One of the goals of childhood and adolescence is to be able to name the feelings we are experiencing. It's one of the responsibilities of parents to teach 'the feeling language' to their children. The goal for us as adults is to consistently remain loving, compassionate and detached, together with all the rest of the virtues, regardless of any negative feelings or thoughts, but monitoring them so we can remain in our spiritual reality.

Here is an example of teaching the 'feeling language'. My sister Kathryn and her three year old daughter, Natalie, were visiting us one Christmas holiday. Unexpectedly, Natalie came screaming into the living room and jumped into her mother's arms. None of us knew why. But her mother did. Natalie had heard a helicopter above the house. She was terrified of helicopters.

Her mother calmly said, 'Natalie, tell Mama, "I feel afraid because of the helicopter." Tell Mama "I'm afraid and worried"!'

My sister was teaching Natalie to connect the 'event' with the 'feelings' she had about it. She was teaching her the language of feelings. There are more than 250 words for feelings in the English language.

In reality, ALL of us have SOME of these negative feelings and vain imaginings listed in the table above because we may not have been taught a feeling language and therefore are not able to recognize our feelings and name them. This is why it is necessary to monitor our thoughts and feelings, especially when we are going into 'different territory' and beyond with those who may be mentally ill, physically challenged, wounded, strange to us, unsociable, domineering, imperfect or unable to express themselves clearly.

Please don't feel judged or offended by the illustration of our lower nature. We all have a lower nature; we all fight against lower nature behaviours. The illustration is there to

23

enable us to know exactly how to identify these negative feelings and vain imaginings in ourselves. We need to know what
they look like so we can bring ourselves to account each day.
The positive meditation illustrations are there to support us in
overcoming our fears.

In the next story we learn about a man who could not
control his feelings of rage.

Story 5

# I Do It for the Sake of God

There was a man who suffered the effects of schizophrenia. He could not get along with others. He was in a rage all the time and others were afraid of him because they could not understand him. The man had a beautiful voice, however, and liked to sing in the church choir. For some reason, he could maintain stability while he was performing with the choir in church on Sundays.

His doctor happened to go to the same church and was puzzled that his patient showed none of his symptoms during the choral presentation. One day after many weeks of observation the doctor asked him, 'How are you able to do this when you cannot do so during the rest of your daily life?'

The man answered simply, 'I do it for the sake of God!'

℘

This story illustrates the workings of the Holy Spirit in this man's life. We are told that whatever mental disabilities we suffer, our soul is whole and healthy and unaffected.

Very little is as yet known about the mind and its workings. But one thing is certain: Bahá'ís can and do receive a very remarkable help and protection in this world, one which often surprises their doctors very much![25]

It is very hard to be subject to any illness, particularly a mental one. However, we must always remember these illnesses have nothing to do with our spirit or our inner relation to God. It is a great pity that as yet so little is really known of the mind, its workings and the illnesses that afflict it; no doubt, as the world becomes more spiritually minded and scientists understand the true nature of man, more humane and permanent cures for mental diseases will be found . . .

You must always remember, no matter how much you or your others may be afflicted with mental troubles and the crushing environment of these State Institutions, that your spirit is healthy, near to our Beloved, and will in the next world enjoy a happy and normal state of soul. Let us hope in the meantime scientists will find better and permanent cures for the mentally afflicted. But in this world such illness is truly a heavy burden to bear![26]

Science has progressed a great deal since Shoghi Effendi wrote this in 1948. The good news is that scientists *have* found better, and in some cases permanent, ways of helping the mentally afflicted overcome their symptoms!

Until science can advance further, we need to focus on unity as we seek to create a working intimacy with the mentally ill, casting off fear. Not all of us will be capable, not all of us are called, but perhaps with guidance more of us will be encouraged to try.

Story 6

# The Physically Disabled

I spent five years in intimacy with the physically disabled. It revealed my capacity to love but it also revealed my ignorance and preconceived notions about the disabled.

I was teaching creative writing for the Rockford Area Arts Council and I had a group of five adult students. One of my students typed with his nose. Another pointed to letters and words on an alphabet board he wore over his wheelchair and dictated his story to me one letter or word at a time. Two others could write by hand on the tables on their wheelchairs and the fifth had a computer that anticipated her thoughts when she slapped one of four pods on her desk with her uncontrollable hand, arm and body. Three of my students could not speak.

All these remarkable men and women were highly intelligent, interested in the world around them and wrote between five and seven books each. They proudly sold their books to family and friends who were amazed at the depth of their experiences.

I learned that even though some of them could not communicate verbally and looked and sounded different owing to cerebral palsy, polio or other disabilities, they were astonishingly savvy, loving and service-minded. I wondered, 'How would they be accepted in our Bahá'í community, which has not had my experience?'

The woman who used her computer with four pods was selected as a pioneer for a new computer developed by engineers at the University of Wisconsin. Thousands more people who were challenged were helped because of her intellectual ability to absorb their newly-created program. This opened up a new world for her and even her parents were amazed at the depth of her knowledge and ability. They learned that she was intact, whole and healthy inside her uncontrollable body as she was able to finally communicate with them.

I have a friend who was worried that his ten month old baby was going to be viewed as backward because he continuously rolled his head back and forth in his stroller. When I told this to my class, my student who wrote with her computer laughed because she cannot control the fact that her head rolls back and forth. She made the entire class laugh by demonstrating it. We all know she is not backward. This illustrates our ignorance when we view someone who is differently abled.

Story 7

# The Power of Prayer

A Bahá'í dedicated to her family had an experience of using urgent, passionate prayer that culminated in a miracle.

Her youngest brother was in a horrible automobile accident in California. There was a woman in the Jeep with him. They had been drinking and using drugs that evening. The Jeep was engulfed in flames when it crashed and he kept trying to get that woman out, even though it was apparent that she had been killed instantly.

This is the story the Bahá'í tells about her brother and the power of prayer.

People at the scene pulled at my brother because they knew the vehicle was going to explode any minute but he resisted. Finally, he told me later, there was a force that threw him away from the Jeep just before it exploded.

After the police spoke with him and it became apparent that he was going to be arrested and charged, he left town. He moved to northern Minnesota to hide for a year or so.

After a time he began to turn to God, giving up drugs and alcohol. He began to attend church on Sundays and prayer meetings and Bible study groups. Once he had confidence that the pastor would not judge him, he told him the whole story, ending with the fact that he wanted to put all this behind him.

He called me during this time of isolation and loneliness for his family.

Eventually the California police tracked my brother to Minnesota. The governor of California signed extradition papers so that he could be returned there. Though he was terrified, my brother placed his trust in a merciful God.

When he arrived in California in March, the police told him that he was facing 17 years of imprisonment. They asked him if he had been driving. He said he didn't know because he had been drinking that night. They asked him if the woman was driving. He answered that he couldn't imagine that he would have let her drive because she had a mental disability. His lawyer told him that he had just ruined his chances of winning the case by saying that. The lawyer asked him to plead guilty but he refused because he didn't know the truth.

I began to pray. My mother prayed. My aunt prayed.

In April the prosecution told him that if he pleaded guilty his years of incarceration would be reduced from 17 to 12 to 15. He refused. His lawyers continued trying to build a case.

I prayed in earnest. My brother continued to pray and read his Bible daily.

In May the prosecution offered him new terms and fewer years if he pleaded guilty. He refused again. He wanted to fire his lawyer. I told him to hang on and stay with his lawyer.

That night I set my alarm clock for midnight and got up to say the Tablet of Aḥmad and the Long Healing Prayer, beseeching God to shower His mercy and bounties upon my brother. Night after night I arose at midnight for urgent, tearful, passionate prayer. This was my time that I spent with my brother in jail.

Within one month, in June, his lawyers hired a nationally recognized expert in accident investigation. This man went to the scene of the accident, examined the pictures of every angle of the accident and the point of impact. He concluded that whoever was behind the wheel of the Jeep would have been killed instantly. The woman had been killed instantly.

I continued arising at midnight and praying fervently, single-mindedly for my brother. I began chanting the two prayers instead of just reciting them.

In July my brother's lawyer found a movie based on a true story in which the passenger in a car accident was thrown into the driver's seat upon impact, just as had happened to my brother.

Unrelentingly, I begged deliverance for my brother.

On 15 August they found an eyewitness who had seen the woman driving the Jeep just moments before the accident! At my brother's next court appearance the judge told him that he would be sentenced to two years, minus the time he had already served, which was nine months. The judge felt compelled to sentence him to two years because it was discovered that he had been arrested for drunken driving twice in California and should have known enough to change his behaviour and get help for his addiction to alcohol and drugs. Had he done so, he would not have participated in the behaviours that led to the accident and the death of the woman. He was therefore held to be complicit in her death.

To this day my brother has been faithful to the promises he has made to God and his life has been completely turned around. He remains a student of the Bible, a living testimony to those around him of a prayer answered and an inspiration to those who come into contact with him. His family's commitment to beseeching God provides strong evidence of the power of prayer.

The miracle of this experience is that I have a brother who is now strong and healthy and beautiful and who demonstrates the meaning of yet another of Bahá'u'lláh's Hidden Words:

O My Servant! Thou art even as a finely tempered sword concealed in the darkness of its sheath and its value hidden from the artificer's knowledge. Wherefore come forth from the sheath of self and desire that thy worth may be made resplendent and manifest unto all the world.[27]

I am grateful that my heart calls me to prayer for I have experienced joy through all of these trials. Bahá'u'lláh's son, 'Abdu'l-Bahá, gives us confidence in the act and results of prayer:

> Praise be to God, thy heart is engaged in the commemoration of God, thy soul is gladdened by the glad tidings of God and thou art absorbed in prayer. The state of prayer is the best of conditions, for man is then associating with God. Prayer verily bestoweth life, particularly when offered in private and at times, such as midnight, when freed from daily cares.[28]

And the Universal House of Justice advises us:

> Have faith and confidence, that the Power of the Holy Spirit will flow through you, the right way will appear, the door will open, the right message, the right principle or the right book will be given to you.[29]

Story 8

# Encounter with a Sorrowing Heart

I can't imagine anything as difficult to bear as the loss of an infant. My daughter had an ectopic pregnancy and was haemorrhaging internally. Week after week she had been spotting and was alarmed because she didn't know the cause. Then came the day that the pregnancy had to be terminated. I stayed with her for two weeks to keep house for her and to cook and to hold her.

Words don't come easily. Or rather, the right words don't come easily. How often we want to say something comforting or to acknowledge grief but we show insensitivity. At this crucial moment I didn't want to say something inappropriate. I simply wanted to be responsive and acknowledge her pain. I did this by listening to her, by not trying to fix the pain, by giving her my total attention, by giving her time alone with her husband, by performing many deeds of love.

The months passed and it was approaching the time when the baby would have been born. She called me and told me, in tears, that she didn't know how she would get through that period.

I simply said, 'I don't know how you will either.'

And she gave me a great compliment. 'Oh, Mom, you are so genuine!'

I was astonished! But then, I had responded to her. I had not tried to fix the pain. I simply acknowledged it. I entered her reality rather than imposing my reality upon her. Then my husband and I flew out to the coast to honour the loss of our grandchild on the day she would have been born.

Story 9

# The Power of Faith

In my research on 'mercy' I was to learn that it is the Holy Spirit that helps us to develop merciful susceptibilities. The following story comes from Jermaine, who has seen his brother Keyonte go from trial to trial in an effort to cope with a devastating life. Keyonte's first thought of suicide came when he was six years old as an attempt to end the punishment meted out by an authoritarian father and his wicked friends who continuously tormented and teased him into a rage. Jermaine had to hide his little brother in the closet when his father came home drunk so that he would avoid a beating filled with hatred. Keyonte's inner demons took over in his adult years, pushing him to mercilessly sabotage himself. Jermaine, who is not without his own troubles, shares his own pain here.

When my brother attempted suicide for the fifth known time, I rushed to the hospital and saw him hooked up to an artificial respirator. I prayed that he would make it. I prayed that he would forgive me for my petty grudges. And even in this debilitating state I saw that he radiated the love of God. Instead of the white pallor of death, I saw a ruddy, rosy countenance that assured me that he would live.

Suddenly he vomited all over me and I wept. I went home to change clothes and the minute I opened the door, the phone rang. It was my son-in-law telling me that my daughter had been listed as a missing person.

I was already in a state of shock, still covered with my brother's black, life-giving charcoal vomit! How could I endure this

34

double blow? It was too much. My mind raced in all directions, unable to focus because reason fails you at a time like this. I called friends for support, and though I was calm on the outside, though I was sustained by the power of faith, my hair began falling out by the handful. But for my faith in God I would have fallen. But for the writings of Bahá'u'lláh and His son 'Abdu'l-Bahá I would have lost my conviction that God showers His bounties upon us continually and that we are not to become hopeless under any circumstances.

I remembered that two weeks prior to this double calamity I was in attendance at a Native American sweat. I told those who were conducting it that I had a breathing problem and didn't think I could last the two hours that it might take to conclude the sweat. One of the Bahá'í friends suggested that I could assist outside the sweat lodge by praying. I decided to pray the Tablet of Aḥmad during this period. I recited it 27 times during the length of the sweat, feeling I was contributing to the benefit of those involved.

Looking back, I believe that this experience prepared me for the coming calamities and, indeed, brought them to a head, paving the way for healing. As Bahá'u'lláh comforts us:

> O Son of Man! My calamity is My providence, outwardly it is fire and vengeance, but inwardly it is light and mercy. Hasten thereunto that thou mayest become an eternal light and an immortal spirit. This is My command unto thee, do thou observe it.[30]

My brother survived, and though all his physical resources were depleted, he turned to God and has given up alcohol and drugs to this very day, for which we are all grateful. God turned his life around. And my daughter called home within two weeks to let us know she was okay. Thank God she was safe! I reassured her that I loved her and would support her throughout any difficulty.

Though Jermaine was in a state of fear and felt hopeless, his faith in God sustained him and he saw the plan of God unfolding in his brother's unstable life and in his daughter's life. How many of us could withstand this kind of pressure? What were the virtues granted by the Holy Spirit? I think we could all agree that constancy of hope was something that Jermaine had to strive for, as well as a firm belief that God was going to enable these two loved ones to transform.

Story 10

# Encounter with a Wounded Soul

Some of us are put off by or do not know how to respond to those who carry wounds from childhood well into their adult years. Even for this situation, the writings of Bahá'u'lláh carry the balm of healing, as the next story illustrates.

The travel teacher in this story enters the reality of the suffering soul, not pressing her to forgive her mother, nor telling her that if she just prayed hard enough she would overcome her bitterness and rage, things that would increase the young woman's belief that no one understands her and would be perceived as criticism. Instead, the travel teacher offers a spiritual look at whose child the young woman really is – God's – and the bounties that come from that heritage.

'Why did you birth me when you did not love me?' She screamed it at me.

I was travel teaching and she had asked for a moment of consultation. She was demonstrating how she had confronted her mother. Her emotions were raw and current. Her mother had debased her verbally and physically all her life. And although she was now in her thirties, her mother continued this verbal assault.

She screamed again in anguish, 'Why did she birth me when she did not love me?' desperately wanting an answer.

I hugged her as she sobbed, patting that child who had felt abandoned all her life. I listened to the rage and bitterness that exploded from decades of wanting acknowledgment from the woman she couldn't call 'mother'.

എ

Perhaps you, too, have felt that abandonment and that poignant question rising up from the core of your being. One of the books I always travel with is *Tablets of Bahá'u'lláh*. In one of the Tablets in it He reveals, 'Know thou moreover that all else besides Him have been created through the potency of a word from His presence . . .'[31]

I told her she was created because of God's love. Her mother's body was but a vessel, a receptacle that carried her to birth. A word from God's presence had called her into being, as it had all creatures on earth.

There is much in Bahá'u'lláh's Revelation that nurtures those who have felt abandoned. In the Persian section of the Hidden Words, Bahá'u'lláh addresses us as 'O Son of Bounty!'[32] Those who have been abandoned are considered a son of bounty? I know it seems strange to those of us who usually read the Word of God literally instead of symbolically. But let's go further:

Out of the wastes of nothingness, with the clay of My command I made thee to appear . . .[33]

We are accustomed to a literal understanding of the Genesis account of creation but here Bahá'u'lláh is using a metaphor: 'the clay of my command'. In an Arabic verse from the same book, He states,

With the hands of power I made thee and with the fingers of strength I created thee; and within thee have I placed the essence of My light.[34]

This, after having addressed us as 'O Son of Being!'[35] Beingness is not connected to physicality but to spirit. Again, God called us into being as a spiritual reality and placed the essence of His light within us, out of His love.

I have attended a multitude of Child Abuse Prevention con-
ferences. Picking and choosing among them, I have come to
the understanding that there are three basic promises – three
reasons for hope – that parents and children can count on.
This woman's story is a classic demonstration that the history,
knowledge and experience of both parent and child need to
be addressed.

At one conference I sat in a classroom being taught by an
educator who had won national awards, one from the presi-
dent of the United States, for a programme he had developed
to teach parents how to parent through nurturing. His wife
and infant son were present. When he asked for questions at
the end of his presentation, one woman asked him, 'Now that
you are the father of a six month old son, what kind of parent
do you think you will be?' This man, with all his knowledge
and experience and awards, gave a very humble response. He
said, 'The most I can expect would be to raise a child that
would be treatable by the system should something go wrong.'

This shows that even under the best of circumstances we
cannot have certitude because there are so many variables.
This, then, becomes the first hope for parents, that if a professional can say this, we, too, can humbly do our best with the
knowledge that we can acquire.

The second hope that I learned from another Child Abuse
Prevention conference is that if a child has even one advocate
during his lifetime, he can make it through his difficulties.
And many of us have multitudes of advocates. I can count
five or six in my own childhood. Such an advocate may be
an English teacher, a neighbour, an aunt; or someone who
stood up for us in a time of need, showed us special attention,
gave us an unexpected gift, said a kind word in a moment of
despair. Such a person may not even have known that he or
she has kindled a spark of hope within us.

This brings us back to the Hidden Words, in which He
writes:

Thus, ere thou didst issue from thy mother's womb, I destined for thee two founts of gleaming milk, eyes to watch over thee, and hearts to love thee.[36]

We can look at this literally or symbolically. One meaning could be that we will be provided for either by our mothers and fathers or by a multitude of advocates for children in a larger village, thereby making us sons of 'bounty'. God's bounty extends far beyond our parents.

Then Bahá'u'lláh says:

And My purpose in all this was that thou mightest attain My everlasting dominion and become worthy of My invisible bestowals.[37]

This suggests that Bahá'u'lláh's words are not to be taken in a purely literal sense. We are sons of bounty in His invisible world and everlasting dominion, which is not a physical world.

There is a third reason for hope. I learned that a child can tell if a parent is trying even 51 per cent of the time, and since God's bounty extends far beyond our parents, children learn to gravitate towards that which is healing, nourishing and nurturing . . . and they find it more than 51 per cent of the time. The reason I am alive is because of God's bounty in bringing me healing, nourishment and nurturing more than 51 per cent of the time and making me conscious of it.

Many of us feel as though we are or were failures as parents but when asked what per cent we feel we are giving to our children, it far exceeds 75! It's not easy being a parent. It's not easy growing up in a household where parents have not been educated in nurturing, where they lack the means to care for their children or to provide a spiritual education. But 'Abdu'l-Bahá, in one of His most powerful statements, writes:

Never lose thy trust in God. Be thou ever hopeful, for the

bounties of God never cease to flow upon man. If viewed from one perspective they seem to decrease, but from another they are full and complete. Man is under all conditions immersed in a sea of God's blessings. Therefore, be thou not hopeless under any circumstances, but rather be firm in thy hope.[38]

After waiting decades for a positive response from her mother, the woman in this story is reunited with her mother, who now prays every day . . . a complete turn-around in less than a year. Can you imagine? They chat together and meet for lunch! Vindictiveness and vilification have changed to love, bitterness to forgiveness. An earliest childhood hope fulfilled, as 'Abdu'l-Bahá promised.

What was it that caused this change? Was it a shift in the young woman's perspective because she heard me state these three reasons for hope, combined with Bahá'u'lláh's Revelation? And because she perceived differently, did she feel differently and thereby act differently, causing a different response in her mother? Or was it the knowledge that she was personally called into being through 'a word from His presence' and did this knowledge reassure her of her inherent nobility? I will never know but I will always trust in the power of hope and the Word of God.

Know thou, moreover, that the Word of God – exalted be His glory – is higher and far superior to that which the senses can perceive, for it is sanctified from any property or substance. It transcendeth the limitations of known elements and is exalted above all the essential and recognized substances. It became manifest without any syllable or sound and is none but the Command of God which pervadeth all created things. It hath never been withheld from the world of being. It is God's all-pervasive grace, from which all grace doth emanate. It is an entity far removed above all that hath been and shall be.[39]

That's how powerful the Word of God is. Even if you catch only a phrase of it, it is transformative. This is why the Word of God is so valuable at addressing the issues of the day in which we live.

# Encounter with Another Culture

## Criticism in the Community

When, without loving discernment, we give ourselves the freedom to speak what we think is the whole truth about what we see, we will find a lack of love as well as a lack of truth. This is because there is a larger picture which includes variables and nuances of both capacity and lack of capacity, development, lack of development, family baggage, lack of consciousness. There are also youth, age, health, internal intention and God's Will, rather than simply right or wrong. Actually, the truth is not always manifested. Sometimes it is hidden and can only be found by showing grace, love, courtesy and wisdom during intimacy with those whom we're tempted to criticize.

## The Barrier to Intimacy

### Hidden Criticism: The Roots of Gossip and Backbiting

We might be tempted to criticize when vast numbers of people from diverse cultures settle into our communities as it will be impossible to understand thousands of habits, needs and traditions that challenge the comfortable standards that we have achieved in our Bahá'í communities and have not yet had to rise above. It stands to reason that if we do not criticize others, we have nothing about which to gossip and backbite.

❧

I was visiting a state park, walking down a serene pathway, when I saw a group of Asian adults methodically picking and cutting medicinal plants, and plants that can be used in Asian cooking, and putting them into their baskets. I stopped to talk to them and tried to explain that it is illegal to take plants out of a state park. It angered me to see that they were doing it and I wanted to 'enlighten' them. Their lack of the English language was a barrier.

I walked some distance away and then looked back over my shoulder to see them continuing to cut the plants. I breathed a sigh and then continued my walk through the state park. I realized that I wasn't going to change their reality and decided to leave rather than approach them again. There were also 'cultural' differences that I could not change and should not judge or criticize and I had to accept that.

What virtues did this woman use? Grace is a prominent one. Understanding others and suspending judgement helped her walk away from the situation. Nor did she gossip or complain about this ethnic group to others. She also showed patience because she realized that this group of gatherers could not speak English and therefore this was not the appropriate time to try to correct them or guide them. At the time, she didn't realize that she might be colluding with them in breaking the law by walking away. Stopping to talk with them was an attempt to make sure they did not get arrested or fined. She realized that she would be doing them a favour by assisting them to understand the law of the land but could not get beyond the language barrier. It is hard to know which virtue should trump which in any given situation. This is something we struggle with as Bahá'ís – in this situation both approaches could be said to be virtuous; had she shown more patience in trying to speak with them, she might have prevented them from falling foul of the law. However, her power of discernment helped her to not judge negatively in this situation and to forego criticism.

Therefore, we must exercise extreme patience, sympathy and love toward all mankind, considering no soul as rejected.[40]

Then he becomes just and kind to all humanity; he entertains prejudice and ill will toward none; he shuns no nation or people.[41]

The National Spiritual Assembly of Canada addressed the issue of backbiting and criticism in a letter written in 1969:

We want to speak to you this month on a subject, which despite its negative aspects, is of very great importance in the development of a Bahá'í community. This subject is the widespread social disease which Bahá'u'lláh calls 'backbiting'.

The great difficulty in all such matters is to 'see with His eyes' and not with your own. As the Physician of the soul, the Manifestation of God not only re-creates moral values, but sets these values in a new scale of priorities which correspond to our deepest spiritual needs. It is to be expected that this scale of values will be different from the ones in which non-Bahá'í society has trained our individual consciences. Our spiritual development depends on our willingness to gradually detach ourselves from the standards of the past, however eternal or 'right' these standards may seem, and to make the new standard a part of our inmost beings.

Most of you are familiar with the extremely severe words which Bahá'u'lláh uses in prohibiting backbiting. He says that it is a spiritual blight which 'quenches the light of the heart and extinguishes the life of the soul'. There are only one or two other subjects about which He spoke with such severity. What we must bear in mind is that these words are not a threat; rather they represent the urgent advice of the Divine Physician who alone 'perceiveth the disease and prescribeth the remedy'. He is telling us that, whatever the various spiritual diseases of our times may be, there are some diseases

45

that are fatal, and our greatest danger lies in ignorance.

It is not only the individual who is threatened by backbiting. In a society like the Bahá'í community, which is based on unity, the effect of continued criticism of others is to destroy the very essence of community life. The power of the Bahá'í Cause is that, out of love for Bahá'u'lláh, we willingly suspend our inbred suspicion of our fellow men. By doing so, we permit our fellow believers to become the spiritual beings they really are. It is this process which backbiting attacks. Like certain drugs which are said to affect the genetic code within the cells of the body, backbiting dissolves the mutual trust on which community life depends.

Perhaps the most damaging of all the many forms which backbiting takes is criticism of Bahá'í institutions. The faith of the believers in their national and local assemblies is the breath of life to these central organs of the community. Ultimately, our success in establishing Bahá'u'lláh's Kingdom on earth will depend on our capacity to commit ourselves heart and soul to the decisions of these divinely-guided institutions.

Obviously, we cannot hope to cure ourselves overnight, particularly not in a society like the present one. Nor does the answer lie in a campaign of mutual censure. Rather, we are called upon to begin gently, patiently, lovingly, but firmly and persistently to train our private consciences.

Essentially, backbiting is criticism of others. It is irrelevant whether the criticism is true or untrue. It is equally irrelevant whether or not the criticism was maliciously intended. What causes the damage is criticism itself. [42]

## The Power of Discernment

To replace criticism as a response to others, I propose using the 'power of discernment', which is made up of six components:

1) Self-disclosure, which encourages others to disclose

This is not meant to be a community-wide disclosure but only one on one or with a trusted friend or the local spiritual assembly in the spirit of consultation and for the purpose of creating awareness and spiritual intimacy.

It is also not meant to be a confession of sin for which you desire forgiveness.

2) Entering their reality, in powerlessness, courtesy and trust . . . simply listening quietly

3) Acknowledgment of their reality.

Acknowledgment does not mean endorsement.

See examples of acknowledgement below in chapter 14, entitled Creating Intimacy.

4) Righteous praise of their virtues and the qualities that are present

5) Becoming a servant to them: provide nurturing experiences and pray for them

6) Understand the uplifting qualities inherent in the power of discernment:

- It creates a tranquil consciousness in the hearer because it is offered with praise instead of judgement or disapproval.

- It confirms us on our true path by helping us focus on our internal intentions, which are connected with our gifts.

- It acknowledges the skill that is manifest to create awareness of the skill that is hidden.

- It looks at the need that is manifest in unconscious, self-destructive behaviour to make conscious the power that is hidden or undeveloped.

- It encourages inherent but hidden abilities and powers.

- It creates expansion of consciousness and fearlessness.

# 12

# Entering the Reality of Others

We have to understand the spiritual drama that is ongoing in the lives of each of the seekers coming into the Faith, whether they have been oppressed, whether they are in crisis, whether they are mentally ill. We have to be willing to enter and participate in that drama, their reality, with its accompanying belief system, without criticism and judgement of it. This belief system will not go away simply because they read the writings and pray. Accompaniment in someone else's difficult journey requires daily intimacy, daily contact, daily establishing of trust, daily risk, daily follow up, daily commitment and daily affirmation of their inherent worth.

If we make an attempt at unity and then walk out of the spiritual drama in judgement of the honest and vast, uncontrollable spectrum of life experience across widely different peoples, cultures, times and places, then we cling to our ignorance, preconceived notions, habits and traditions, forgoing the knowledge of God and humankind. And we are the poorer.

Juliet Thompson had a glimpse of how 'Abdu'l-Bahá viewed the troubled when she visited Him in 'Akká and He said:

Our real happiness is of the Kingdom. Here we seek no happiness, because in this world happiness does not exist. If you consider, you will see that people are all in trouble. The majority of people whom you question have nothing to tell you but of their troubles! Their hearts are not at rest. And they cannot have this rest of heart but through the Love of God. Therefore we must know that happiness exists in the other world and not in this.[43]

This is what I mean by the vast, uncontrollable spectrum of reality. Ponder the following questions that illustrate the troubles, tests and difficulties of people who may become attracted to the Faith.

- Can you enter the reality of a person with a disability without offending him or her?

- Can you enter the reality of a man or woman who has chosen prostitution as a way of acting out his or her childhood trauma?

- Can you enter the reality of someone who has been sexually abused?

- Can you enter the reality of someone who has suffered racial abuse?

- Can you enter the reality of someone who is suffering from addictions such as alcohol, drugs, sex, work, exercise or money?

- Can you enter the reality of someone who expresses his or her anger passive-aggressively?

- Do you know how to set a boundary with someone who is passive/aggressive when you are tempted to give up and abandon him or her?

- Do you know how to enter the reality of someone who is angry without becoming defensive, converting, fixing or judging and becoming totally logical to try to control the situation in order to 'help' them change?

- Do you know how to listen, without losing patience, to someone who keeps repeating the same lifetime grudges every time you meet with him or her?

- Do you know how to set boundaries and limits to reduce your own stress?

- Do you know how to instantly help someone save face?

- Can you show grace at irreverence or at reverence that is less reverent than yours, or at disorderly reverence or at an absolute lack of knowledge of worship?

- Can you sit outside a Feast or fireside with someone who is terrified of the community and sitting on the front porch is the closest he or she can come to participating?

- Can you be alert to a person's hyper-vigilance and discreetly ask 'What's wrong?' 'How can I help you right now?' 'What do you need right now?' instead of ignoring his or her anxiety and going back in to worship?

- Can you ask the person, 'How did you come to that belief?' and listen for an hour without offering an alternative belief?

- Can you tolerate the kind of inconsistent commitment that sees a person change his or her mind every 15 minutes so you never know from day to day what kind of reception you're going to have when you go to pick up a person for a Feast or fireside?

- Will you be willing to take a person home immediately if he changes his mind about being there 15 minutes after you arrive at the Feast or fireside?

- Can you smell body odour, bad breath and house odour up close in your face for ten years without criticizing?

- Would you be willing to attend a support group for family members of the mentally ill?

There is no preconceived formula that will meet all the needs of people whose lives prompt the questions I've posed here. However, it behoves every community to consult on these and similar questions so that it is prepared for the uncontrollable spectrum of life experience that is soon to enter our communities.

> Let it not be imagined that expedience is the essential motive arousing this sense of urgency. There is an overarching reason: it is the pitiful plight of masses of humanity, suffering and in turmoil, hungering after righteousness, but 'bereft of discernment to see God with their own eyes, or hear His Melody with their own ears'. They must be fed. Vision must be restored where hope is lost, confidence built where doubt and confusion are rife.[44]

> But when you find a person living up to the teachings of Bahá'u'lláh, following the precepts of the Hidden Words, know that he belongs to Bahá'u'lláh; and, verily, I proclaim that he is of me. If, on the other hand, you see anyone whose deeds and conduct are contrary to and not in conformity with the good pleasure of the Blessed Perfection and against the spirit of the Hidden Words, let that be your standard and criterion of judgement against him, for know that I am altogether severed from him no matter who he may be. This is the truth.[45]

This is a 'promise and a warning' for us to live by the teachings of Bahá'u'lláh no matter how advanced, ignorant, mentally ill or unspiritual people in our community are or may seem. As we do not know the secrets of their hearts, it is best to suspend judgement.

In the Bahá'í Cause arts, sciences and all crafts are (counted as) worship. The man who makes a piece of notepaper to the best of his ability, conscientiously, concentrating all his forces on perfecting it, is giving praise to God. Briefly, all effort and exertion put forth by man from the fullness of his heart is worship, if it is prompted by the highest motives and the will to do service to humanity. This is worship: to serve mankind and to minister to the needs of the people. Service is prayer. A physician ministering to the sick, gently, tenderly, free from prejudice and believing in the solidarity of the human race, he is giving praise.[46]

'Abdu'l-Bahá counsels us:

O ye friends of God! Show ye an endeavour that all the nations and communities of the world, even the enemies, put their trust, assurance and hope in you; that if a person falls into errors for a hundred-thousand times he may yet turn his face to you, hopeful that you will forgive his sins; for he must not become hopeless, neither grieved nor despondent. This is the conduct and the manner of the people of Bahá. This is the foundation of the most high pathway! Ye should conform your conduct and manners with the advices of 'Abdu'l-Bahá.[47]

But He also warns us:

O ye beloved of the Lord! The Kingdom of God is founded upon equity and justice, and also upon mercy, compassion, and kindness to every living soul. Strive ye then with all your heart to treat compassionately all humankind – except for those who have some selfish, private motive, or some disease of the soul. Kindness cannot be shown the tyrant, the deceiver, or the thief, because, far from awakening them to the error of their ways, it maketh them to continue in their perversity as before. No matter how much kindliness ye may expend upon the liar, he will but lie the more, for he believeth you to be deceived, while ye understand him but too well, and only remain silent out of your extreme compassion.[48]

Try not to confuse the sometimes 'defensive' behaviour of the mentally ill with the qualities of those who have 'some selfish, private motive or some disease of the soul'. They are not the same things. With careful observation over a period of time and deeper acquaintance, a person's spiritual reality will become evident.

The bestowals of God which are manifest in all phenomenal life are sometimes hidden by intervening veils of mental and mortal vision which render man spiritually blind and incapable, but when those scales are removed and the veils rent asunder, then the great signs of God will become visible, and he will witness the eternal light filling the world. The bestowals of God are all and always manifest. The promises of heaven are ever present. The favours of God are all-surrounding, but should the conscious eye of the soul of man remain veiled and darkened, he will be led to deny these universal signs and remain deprived of these manifestations of divine bounty.[49]

13

# The Power of the Holy Spirit

Each of the examples that I have worked into this book shows the power of the Holy Spirit and the Word of God. It is clear that the Holy Spirit works towards the good in all the world religions.

If we realized that there is no 'us' and 'them' based on differences of religion, race, ethnic group, mental health, physical ability or wounding, and if we understood that the Holy Spirit is cosmic, working through all the Holy Books that have been sent to us by God through the Holy Revelators, we would cling to the Word of God and keep God's Covenant as never before in the hope of developing the virtues we need to serve in capacities we never thought possible. All we have to do is trust, believe and watch for confirmations.

We cannot assume, based on our unexamined perceptions, that the Holy Spirit is not nurturing all of those whom we do not understand and refuse to hold close in our communities. As 'Abdu'l-Bahá has reminded us, we should look at a person's ONE GOOD quality and love his or her spiritual reality!

Think first of the spiritual reality of those who are confused, wounded, mentally ill or physically challenged with no voice or without an advocate. Then act with your spiritual reality and the Holy Spirit will guide you.

> Verily will the consummate power of the Divine Reality breathe into you the bounties of the Holy Spirit, and aid you to perform an exploit whose like the eye of creation hath never looked upon.[50]

Day and night I entreat and supplicate to the Kingdom of God and beg for you infinite assistance and confirmation. Do not take into consideration your own aptitudes and capacities, but fix your gaze on the consummate bounty, the divine bestowal and the power of the Holy Spirit – the power that converteth the drop into a sea and the star into a sun.[51]

Know thou of a certainty that Love is the secret of God's holy Dispensation, the manifestation of the All-Merciful, the fountain of spiritual outpourings. Love is heaven's kindly light, the Holy Spirit's eternal breath that vivifieth the human soul. Love is the cause of God's revelation unto man, the vital bond inherent, in accordance with the divine creation, in the realities of things. Love is the one means that ensureth true felicity both in this world and the next. Love is the light that guideth in darkness, the living link that uniteth God with man, that assureth the progress of every illumined soul. Love is the most great law that ruleth this mighty and heavenly cycle, the unique power that bindeth together the divers elements of this material world, the supreme magnetic force that directeth the movements of the spheres in the celestial realms. Love revealeth with unfailing and limitless power the mysteries latent in the universe. Love is the spirit of life unto the adorned body of mankind, the establisher of true civilization in this mortal world, and the shedder of imperishable glory upon every high-aiming race and nation.[52]

# 14

# Creating Intimacy:

## How to Maintain Intimacy in a Community of Wounded Souls

Intimacy is the ability to enter into connectedness with others without the fear of domination or the desire to dominate. It is the moral integrity to commit to unity of identity collectively without the fear of losing authority of self.[53]

Because unjust authority has shaped our identities, we still fear domination. A history of force, racism, sexism, nationalism, war and many types of mental illness has made us distrust intimacy and power. Our challenge now is how to establish intimacy without force blocking our efforts, as we slowly, and sometimes painfully, exit a paradigm of domination or perceived domination.

Even people who are not mentally ill have difficulty with intimacy, so by peeling away the layers of how we interact in conversations with others, we may be able to achieve the highest level of intimacy and begin to truly understand one another.

### Exercises in the Different Levels of Intimacy

*Getting to Know You! An 'Ice Breaker'*

Five Levels/Aspects of Intimacy

- Self-disclosure by you + acknowledgement by another = awareness

- Self-disclosure by the other + acknowledgement by you
  = greater awareness

The following is but one model for explaining intimacy. There are five distinct levels of intimacy.

1) The lowest level is information: 'I live in Rockford, Illinois. I was born in 1941. I like the colour blue.'

   We discover things about each other when we exchange this type of basic information. However, we do not really get to know one another.

*Exercise:*

- Tell your partner where you live, when you were born, what colour you like. Stay with the facts only, nothing more. Continue to exchange facts, facts about the room, about the floor, the weather, and so on.

2) The second level of intimacy is the sharing of opinions. This exchange can also be impersonal. I may have an opinion about abortion which I cannot share with someone who has absolute pro-life views. Therefore I cannot go beyond the first level with a pro-life person. I would have to trust that I would not be judged and condemned.

*Exercises:*

- With a partner, share your opinion about abortion.

- With a partner, share your opinion about bullying in school.

- With a partner, share your opinion about the concealed

carry of guns in the United States.

- With a partner, share your opinion about immorality in the media.

3) The third level of intimacy is sharing feelings. If I think that a person could not care less about my feelings, I might think, 'Why bother?' and not make the attempt to engage with him. It is important to note that inability to share feelings with anyone indicates an undeveloped identity.

*Exercises:*

- With a partner, share your feelings about child abuse.

- With a partner, share your feelings about the many wars that are going on in the world right now.

Remember to use feeling words such as anxiety, fear, anger, disillusionment, hopeful, disappointment, joyful, trusting, confusing, up and down.

4) The fourth level of intimacy is sharing my attitude. This is a pretty high level of trust. I am really opening myself up to the judgement and criticism of others with this one, especially with an authoritarian employer or parent. Be aware that 'attitude' can also include gossip about and criticism of others, as well as blaming others.

*Exercises:*

- Talk about a time that you shared your attitude with someone and you wished that you had not? How did you feel? (Example from the author, now 70 years old. 'When I was 15 years old, I asked my mother to wake me up to catch the early bus and she forgot. I said, angrily, 'Mom, you fouled me up!' End result was punishment and shame as a result of her disappointment in me.)

• Share an incident or moment when you had a blaming attitude and then realized that you had to take responsibility. What did you do?

5) The fifth and highest level of intimacy is sharing the personal, spiritual level of my faith, whether my personal belief culled from experience, religion itself or the Bahá'í Faith. This would include that which gives me hope, insight and freedom. It would also reveal my spiritual vulnerability and my powerlessness. The fourth level can prepare us for this higher level, at which we share spiritual principles combined with our personal experiences to create even greater awareness and insight for others and ourselves.

*Exercises:*

• What spiritual principles of the Bahá'í Faith give you hope during this restless period through which humankind is going right now?

• Was there a point at which your faith turned to despair and then you turned to the writings and found something that gave you insight? What was it?

• Was there a time when you felt too restricted by the commandments of God but then, by striving to keep them, you felt even greater freedom than before? Can you share that?

## Models for Acknowledgement

Any endeavour that requires information being transmitted to a listener also requires acknowledgement by the listener. At the end of the Long Obligatory Prayer we are prompted to 'acknowledge' God. We can do no less when listening to the spiritual reality, ideas and beliefs of another human being. The feeling of being understood by someone helps us to trust our partner in conversation. Here are simple ways we can communicate acknowledgement:

- I can appreciate that this belief, idea, perception is very important to you. This is the awareness I have because you have shared it with me. I've never experienced or thought of that before and I'm grateful to you for sharing it with me.

- I appreciate your insights. They help me understand you better.

- Help me understand your life experience better by saying it in a different way.

- That sounds very important to you and therefore it is very important to me. Could you rephrase that so that I can understand you more completely?

- Hearing your viewpoint helps me understand myself better. I accept the differences between us and I can also see the similarities. Thank you for sharing.

In short, we create intimacy through the process of revealing our identity to another human being via these aspects of intimacy; and others, in turn, reveal their identity to us. Surely we Bahá'ís want to achieve the highest level of intimacy with one another, take pride in one another's accomplishments and know the beauty of one another's souls. This is at the heart of Bahá'u'lláh's mission to unite the whole world. 'Abdu'l-Bahá wrote:

> Should one soul from amongst the believers meet another, it must be as though a thirsty one with parched lips has reached to the fountain of the water of life, or a lover has met his true beloved. For one of the greatest divine wisdoms regarding the appearance of the holy Manifestations is this: The souls may come to know each other and become intimate with each other . . . [54]

# Appendix
# Including Notes from Other People

## Mental Disorders

*The Assembly Does Not Have the Role of Therapist*

In every aspect of offering assistance to families or individuals, the assembly must always bear in mind that it cannot, and must not, try to assume the role of therapist for which it is neither mandated nor equipped. It may be helpful in some circumstances, and always with the prior consent of the individual involved, for the assembly to provide general information to a therapist about the teachings of the Bahá'í Faith. While respectful acknowledgement of the feelings, circumstances and perceptions of an individual is an essential component of a productive relationship, ownership and responsibility for the interpretation and resolution of a person's problems must remain with the individual. It is not the assembly's role to interpret, explain, excuse, criticize or solve an individual's problems however sympathetic the members of the assembly may be. It is the responsibility of the individual (or, if the individual is mentally incompetent, the first degree relatives and family members or guardian), within the context of spiritual transformation and, if needed, with the aid of trained professionals and support groups specially constituted for that purpose, to acknowledge, interpret, analyse and resolve his or her own life issues, whatever they may be.

Local assemblies may suggest mental health counselling or support groups but should confine their own work with individuals to issues of personal spiritual transformation, understanding and application of spiritual principles, adherence to Bahá'í laws, functioning within the Bahá'í community and firmness in the Covenant. In some American states, such as California, it is possible that an assembly may be subject to legal action for attempting to provide counselling in cases of mental disorders.

In personal correspondence with me, a friend offered some suggestions relevant to the situation outlined in Story 4 above:

> I was also going to suggest that a study group specifically for the person and daughter with mental issues be set up just for them with the accompaniment of an individual who is capable of being both kind and assertive enough to bring the topic back to the issue if it should wander off track too far. I think it is always important to educate and train those who want it but it can be done in a way that doesn't affect everyone. If new seekers are willing to make allowances for people with mental issues, then it is well worth the effort to include everyone. If, however, interacting with such people would cause problems then there should be enough flexibility to hold separate events for those who need special attention.
>
> At Feast, if the person is willing to be guided by others, then the need to monopolize the conversation may be countered with gentle interruptions. However, if the person is not willing, it may be necessary for someone to ask him or her to go into another room so that the person's issues can be addressed without the consultation being dominated by one person. It takes a strong chair with the support of the entire Assembly for such a method to be effective.
>
> Here are a few other quotes from *Developing Distinctive Bahá'í Communities* with some suggestions, including where additional help can be found.

## *The Assembly is a Spiritual Shepherd*

The divinely ordained institution of the Local Spiritual Assembly operates at the first levels of human society and is the basic administrative unit of Bahá'u'lláh's World Order. It is concerned with individuals and families whom it must constantly encourage to unite in a distinctive Bahá'í society, vitalized and guarded by the laws, ordinances and principles of Bahá'u'lláh's Revelation. It protects the Cause of God; it acts as the loving shepherd of the Bahá'í flock.[55]

In its interactions with an individual who suffers from mental disorder(s), the Assembly and its representatives should strive to be:

- kind without being either indulgent or patronizing

- observant without being either condoning or judging, unless the Assembly is considering a matter that requires a judgement

- detached without being indifferent or lacking in empathy

- assertive about maintaining appropriate boundaries without being aggressive or intrusive

- alert for and prepared to confront domineering, intrusive, manipulative or avoidant behaviours. Such behaviours are often learned in childhood as adaptive, self-protective responses. Carried over into adulthood, they prevent healthy relationships.

- prepared to contact private or public support services, if it appears that the individual might harm him/herself or others

- encouraging and supportive of behaviour that is in keeping with the teachings of the Faith. When necessary, identify and patiently, lovingly, firmly confront and limit behaviour that is contrary to Bahá'í standards. Consistency is important.

Persons experiencing mental disorders may, at times, be emotionally volatile. Assemblies and persons representing Assemblies have a great responsibility to manifest spiritual characteristics regardless of how others behave.[56]

## Suggestions for Possible Assembly Action

It is the responsibility of Bahá'í Assemblies to decide when individual interests should be subordinated to those affecting the collective welfare of the community. But, as already stated, the interest of the individual should always be safeguarded within certain limits, and provided they do not seriously affect the welfare of the group as a whole.[57]

In cases of mental disorders, the Assembly should make its decisions first in consideration of the benefit and welfare of the whole community and then in finding resources for the individual. Assemblies are encouraged to seek advice from local mental health professionals, including social service agencies and qualified non-profit organizations, concerning specific situations and to draw upon these resources in deciding upon any course of action. If the Assembly becomes aware of a problem that might be an indicator of mental illness or other disorder it should avoid suggesting that there might be a mental problem, as it is not qualified to make such a determination. Depending on the circumstances, it may wish to suggest that the person undergo a medical evaluation through his or her primary care physician or other health care practitioner. If individuals with mental disorders are repeatedly writing letters or making phone calls to the

Assembly, it may wish to appoint a liaison with a capacity to listen to interact with the individual. It may be helpful to assist people to clarify and focus their thinking by asking, 'Why are you telling me that?' It is also possible to politely interrupt a flow of monologue that is unproductive.

If the person's problems are affecting the community, the Assembly may wish to establish clear boundaries regarding his or her behaviour in relation to itself, the community and, if necessary, to particular individuals within the community, with explicit consequences for violating the boundaries. If that approach is used:

- Care should be taken to establish boundaries that are reasonable and consequences that are appropriate. If possible, this should be done in consultation and cooperation with the individual involved. The Assembly may find it helpful to put the boundaries and consequences for violating them in the form of a written contract at the time of the agreement so that both the individual and the Assembly will have a copy. If possible, the actual wording should be agreed upon by both the individual and the Assembly. This will help to reduce confusion and minimize individual differences of perception in recalling what was decided when referring to the agreement in the future.

- Once consequences are specified, if the predetermined boundaries are violated, the Assembly must act to impose the consequences. If need for a therapist is indicated, the Assembly may wish to suggest that the person get a referral from his or her primary physician, if they do not already have someone they are seeing or would like to see. If the individual's behaviour seems to be so extreme that immediate assistance is required, the Assembly or its liaison may wish to contact a mental health crisis intervention unit or the police, as seems appropriate to the situation.

Additional advice and insight may be found in *Some Guidance for Spiritual Assemblies Related to Mental Illness and Its Treatment. Suggestions for Encouraging Individuals with Mental Disorders.*

With reference to the broad aspects of your problem of psychological difficulty, the House of Justice has asked us to quote the following passages from the Writings of Bahá'u'lláh: 'Know thou that the soul of man is exalted above, and is independent of all infirmities of body or mind . . . When it (the soul) leaveth the body, however, it will evince such ascendancy, and reveal such influence as no force on earth can equal.' In a letter written on behalf of the beloved Guardian we also find the following passage: 'You must always remember, no matter how much you and others are afflicted with mental troubles . . . that your spirit is healthy, near to your Beloved, and will in the next world enjoy a happy and normal state of soul.' Thus it is that the soul is not aided by psychotherapy. On the other hand, in your understanding of the mental phenomena which distress you, and in your efforts to overcome your problem it is perfectly proper to consult professional experts, as your National Assembly . . . advised. In another letter written on behalf of Shoghi Effendi by his secretary, we read the following: 'As Bahá'u'lláh has urged us to avail ourselves of the help of good physicians, Bahá'ís are certainly not only free to turn to psychiatry for assistance but should, when available, do so.' The mind, then, with all its aberrancies, may often favourably be influenced by scientifically trained persons.

The Universal House of Justice suggests that through daily prayer, and specially by observing the daily obligatory prayers, through study of the Writings, through active participation in teaching efforts and in the activities of the community, and through constant effort to sacrifice for the Faith you love so well, you will provide a spiritual counterpart to the professional help you will receive from the experts. You should also endeavour to engage in some useful occupation, or by training yourself to have such an occupation, as work is itself another means at our disposal, in accordance with our Teachings, to draw nearer to God, and to better grasp His purpose for us in this world.[58]

We need to be conscious of our capacity, individually and as a community. Just as communities must decide how many new people they can responsibly enrol, they need to check their resources to see if they are up to incorporating mentally ill individuals. It can destroy them. How can we best use our limited resources in service to humanity? Seek those with capacity and build on it.[59]

## A Word of Caution

There may be times when medication does not successfully maintain a person who is suffering from a mental illness. In that case, a person who is attempting to assist must know his or her limitations. Just as the Local Spiritual Assembly is not called upon to act as a 'therapist', neither should individuals try to provide therapy. Rather they should rely upon prayer after putting the matter into the hands of a professional. If one sees signs of violence, it is because the individual involved is attempting to cope under very difficult circumstances. The person may experience shame and want privacy while he goes through unexpected changes in his mood and stability. No one expects you to put yourself in danger. Consult with your Local Spiritual Assembly and respectfully honour the individual's privacy and your own limitations.

# Bibliography

'Abdu'l-Bahá. *Paris Talks*. London: Bahá'í Publishing Trust, 1967.

— *The Promulgation of Universal Peace*. Wilmette, IL: Bahá'í Publishing Trust, 1982.

— *Selections from the Writings of 'Abdu'l-Bahá*. Haifa: Bahá'í World Centre, 1978.

— *Some Answered Questions*. Wilmette, IL: Bahá'í Publishing Trust, 1981.

— *Tablets of Abdul-Baha Abbas*. Chicago: Bahá'í Publishing Society, vol. 2, 1915.

— *Tablets of the Divine Plan*. Wilmette, IL: Bahá'í Publishing Trust, 1993.

*Abdul Baha on Divine Philosophy*. Boston: The Tudor Press, 1918.

Babb, Kim. Letter to the Universal House of Justice, 16 January 2005 (never sent).

Bahá'u'lláh. *The Hidden Words*. Wilmette, IL: Bahá'í Publishing Trust, 1990.

— *Kitáb-i-Íqán*. Wilmette, IL: Bahá'í Publishing Trust, 1989.

— *The Seven Valleys and the Four Valleys*. Wilmette, IL: Bahá'í Publishing Trust, 1991.

— *Tablets of Bahá'u'lláh*. Wilmette, IL: Bahá'í Publishing Trust, 1988.

Clarken, Professor Rodney. Personal correspondence, February 2012.

*Diary of Juliet Thompson, The*. Los Angeles: Kalimát Press, 1983.

Interfaith blogspot. http://nccinterfaith.blogspot.com/2006/03/ethics daily publishes my response to.html.

Ives, Howard Colby. *Portals to Freedom*. Oxford: George Ronald, 1973.

*Lights of Guidance: A Bahá'í Reference File*. Compiled by Helen Hornby. New Delhi: Bahá'í Publishing Trust, 5th ed. 1997.

National Spiritual Assembly of the Bahá'ís of Canada. Letter of 1 August 1969.

National Spiritual Assembly of the Bahá'ís of the United States. *Developing Distinctive Bahá'í Communities: Guidelines for Spiritual Assemblies*. Wilmette, IL: National Spiritual Assembly of the Bahá'ís of the United States, rev. ed. 2008. http://venturacountylsa. wikispaces.com/file/view/Developing+Distinctive+Bahai+Commu nities+v6+complete.pdf.

Peterson, Phyllis K. *Assisting the Traumatized Soul: Healing the Wounded Talisman*. Wilmette, IL: Bahá'í Publishing Trust, 1999.

Rabbaní, Rúḥíyyih. *The Priceless Pearl*. London: Bahá'í Publishing Trust, 1969.

Radpour, Mary K. *Some Guidance for Spiritual Assemblies Related to Mental Illness and Its Treatment*. Chattanooga, TN: Images International, 1999.

Rilke, Rainer Maria. *Letters to a Young Poet*. New York: W.W. Norton, rev. ed. 1954.

Shoghi Effendi. *The Advent of Divine Justice*. Wilmette, IL: Bahá'í Publishing Trust, 1990.

— *The World Order of Bahá'u'lláh*. Wilmette, IL: Bahá'í Publishing Trust, 1991.

The Universal House of Justice. Letter to the Conference of the Continental Boards of Counsellors, 27 December 2005.

— *Messages from the Universal House of Justice 1963–1986: The Third Epoch of the Formative Age*. Wilmette, IL: Bahá'í Publishing Trust, 1996.

— *A Wider Horizon: Selected Messages of the Universal House of Justice 1983–1992*. Riviera Beach, FL: Palabra Publications, 1992.

# Notes and References

1. Since, for example, I have a family member who is mentally ill and I experience stress because of my own ignorance about how to assist him, it would behove me to take advantage of a support group for family members. We of the Bahá'í community should do no less!
2. Kim Babb works with autistic children in a school setting.
3. Letter of the Universal House of Justice to the Conference of the Continental Boards of Counsellors, 27 December 2005.
4. Shoghi Effendi, quoted in Rabbaní, *Priceless Pearl.* p. 367.
5. Shoghi Effendi, *Advent of Divine Justice*, p. 54.
6. Shoghi Effendi, *World Order*, p. 41.
7. National Spiritual Assembly of the Bahá'ís of the United States, *Developing Distinctive Bahá'í Communities*, p. 825.
8. Bahá'u'lláh, *Kitáb-i-Íqán*, p. 112.
9. Bahá'u'lláh, *Tablets*, p. 89.
10. 'Abdu'l-Bahá, *Selections*, p. 53.
11. Bahá'u'lláh, *Tablets*, p. 173.
12. Bahá'u'lláh, *Hidden Words*, Arabic no. 25.
13. From a letter of the Universal House of Justice, Riḍván 1989, in the Universal House of Justice, *Wider Horizon*, p. 142.
14. Bahá'u'lláh, Four Valleys, in *Seven Valleys*, pp. 51–2.
15. Rilke, *Letters to a Young Poet*, p. 68.
16. 'Abdu'l-Bahá, *Divine Philosophy*, p. 96.
17. 'Abdu'l-Bahá, *Paris Talks*, p. 60.
18. 'Abdu'l-Bahá, *Some Answered Questions*, p. 118.
19. Ives, *Portals to Freedom*, pp. 84–5.
20. 'Abdu'l-Bahá, *Promulgation*, p. 41.
21. ibid. p. 291.
22. 'Abdu'l-Bahá, *Paris Talks*, pp. 170–1.
23. 'Abdu'l-Bahá, *Promulgation*, p. 40.
24. ibid. p. 63.

25. From a letter written on behalf of Shoghi Effendi to an individual, 9 April 1948, in *Lights of Guidance*, p. 281.
26. From a letter written on behalf of Shoghi Effendi to an individual, 12 April 1948, in *Lights of Guidance*, p. 281.
27. Bahá'u'lláh, *Hidden Words*, Persian no. 72.
28. 'Abdu'l-Bahá, *Selections*, p. 202.
29. Guidance to Ruth Moffat quoted in a letter of the Universal House of Justice to an individual, in the Universal House of Justice, *Messages 1963–1986*, p. 385.
30. Bahá'u'lláh, *Hidden Words*, Arabic no. 51.
31. Bahá'u'lláh, *Tablets*, p. 110.
32. Bahá'u'lláh, *Hidden Words*, Persian no. 29.
33. ibid.
34. ibid. Arabic no. 12.
35. ibid.
36. Bahá'u'lláh, *Hidden Words*, Persian no. 29.
37. ibid.
38. 'Abdu'l-Bahá, *Selections*, p. 205.
39. Bahá'u'lláh, *Tablets*, pp. 140–1.
40. 'Abdu'l-Bahá, *Promulgation*, p. 286.
41. ibid. p. 41.
42. Letter of the National Spiritual Assembly of Canada, 1 August 1969.
43. *Diary of Juliet Thompson*, p. 25.
44. From a letter of the Universal House of Justice, Riḍván 1988, in the Universal House of Justice, *Wider Horizon*, p. 58.
45. 'Abdu'l-Bahá, *Promulgation*, p. 457.
46. 'Abdu'l-Bahá, *Paris Talks*, pp. 176–7.
47. 'Abdu'l-Bahá, *Tablets,* vol. 2, p. 436.
48. 'Abdu'l-Bahá, *Selections*, p. 158.
49. 'Abdu'l-Bahá, *Promulgation*, p. 90.
50. 'Abdu'l-Bahá, *Selections*, p. 85.
51. ibid. p. 104.
52. ibid. p. 27.
53. 'Authority of self' is loosely defined as permission to use all our personal powers in deference to the Covenant of Bahá'u'lláh. For a complete description, see Peterson, *Assisting the Traumatized Soul: Healing the Wounded Talisman.*
54. 'Abdu'l-Bahá, *Tablets of the Divine Plan*, p. 52.
55. From a letter of the Universal House of Justice to the Bahá'ís of

the World, Naw-Rúz 1974, in the Universal House of Justice, *Messages 1963–1986*, no. 141.13, p. 264.

56. National Spiritual Assembly of the Bahá'ís of the United States, *Developing Distinctive Bahá'í Communities,* pp. 827–8.

57. From a letter written on behalf of Shoghi Effendi to an individual, 26 June 1936, in *Lights of Guidance*, p. 121.

58. From a letter written on behalf of the Universal House of Justice to an individual, 6 April 1976, in *Lights of Guidance*, p. 283.

59. Professor Rodney Clarken, personal correspondence, February 2012.